The Triumph of Tradition

How the Resurgence of Religion is Reawakening a Conservative World

Stephen R. Turley, Ph.D.

TURLEY TALKS
A New Conservative Age is Rising
www.TurleyTalks.com

Table of Contents

Acknowledgements

This book originated as a paper I delivered at Patrick Henry College as part of its Faith and Reason lecture series on February 9, 2018. I want to thank particularly President Jack Haye, Stephen Allen, Director of Admission and Communication, and Prof. Mark Mitchell for their kindness and gracious hospitality in hosting me for the day. I would also like to extend my gratitude to the faculty, panelists, and students for their insightful interactions with my paper. I also owe a deep debt of gratitude to my colleagues Dr. Nicholas DiDonato and Dr. David Deiner for their reading and interaction with the paper in its earlier draft form.

The Restoration of Man?

It was February 24th, 1943. Great Britain was in its fourth year of battle in World War II, a conflict that involved, according to then Prime Minister Winston Churchill, nothing less than the survival of Christian civilization. C.S. Lewis, along with his brother Warren, traveled from Oxford to the small medieval town of Durham to deliver three successive talks for The Riddell Memorial Lectures series, which were founded in memory of Sir John Buchanan Riddell, a devout Christian, with the stated intention of exploring the interface between religion and contemporary thought. Lewis' brother Warren wrote in his diary that their visit to Durham was like "a little oasis in the dreariness" of their lives, an escape from the daily food rationing of urban British life in the midst of the war. I can attest firsthand to this oasis; much of my doctoral research was spent in the shadow of Durham's magnificent eleventh-century Norman cathedral at the city-center, its sacred splendor nestled between castle and college.

This cathedral, standing as it was against the dreary beleaguered background of WWII, served an almost parable-like setting for the content of Lewis' lectures over the next three evenings during the university's Epiphany term. The first lecture began simple enough; Lewis addressed the current state of British education, which he saw as eclipsing the classical tradition's emphasis on fostering wisdom and virtue with an exclusive focus on technical competency and scientific utilitarianism. The education "of old" (as he would say) envisioned the world filled with divine meaning and purpose, and thus sought to foster wisdom through a knowledge of this divine meaning and purpose on the one hand, and to cultivate virtue through the right ordering our loves in accordance with this divine economy on the other. In Lewis' words, classical education centered on "the doctrine of objective value, the belief that certain attitudes are really true, and others really false, to the kind of thing the universe is and the kind of things we are."[1] Classical education sought to harmonize what we know with what we love, integrating our intellect and our appetites, exemplified in a life of wisdom and virtue.

However, Lewis observed that modern education, that is, the education that characterized much of mid-20th century Britain, was in effect pulling apart the head from the appetites by redefining knowledge solely in terms of scientifically verified facts. Because it was supposed that facts such as '2 + 2 = 4' are value-free, in that their validity transcends any person's or

---

[1] C.S. Lewis, *The Abolition of Man* (New York: Simon & Schuster, 1975), 31.

culture's value system, they have no moral significance. There is no objective meaning or purpose or moral integrity in the world of facts; there are, well, only facts, nothing more.

In this modern reduction of the world as knowable only through value-free facts, Lewis was concerned that contemporary education was in effect destroying the possibility of cultivating virtue. If virtue involved ordering our loves and organizing our sentiments in accordance with a divinely authored economy of goods, then any denial of such a divine economy in effect negated the very metaphysical basis by which our loves could be ordered. For Lewis, British education was creating a generation of young people cut-off from the objective values of the True, the Good, and the Beautiful, thereby depriving them of the very transcendent means by which their humanity flourished.

But as the lectures developed, it was clear that Lewis was not merely concerned with educational curriculum and pedagogy. For Lewis, these two divergent educational approaches represented nothing less than *two fundamentally different human projects*, what could be considered two fundamentally different ages or civilizations, what we might call the *moral* age versus the *modern* age, the *sapient* versus the *scientific* age.

Lewis summarizes these two ages thusly: For classical man, the fundamental question was: "How do I conform my soul to the world around me and thus be drawn up into divine life?" The answer was through prayer, virtue, and knowledge. However, for modern man, the question is inverted: modern man is not interested in how to conform the soul to reality. Instead modern man asks, "How do I conform the world to my own desires and ambitions?" The answer involves tapping into those institutions that operate by the mechanisms of power and manipulation, namely, science, technology, and the state.

Now what Lewis observes is that these two contrasting visions of reality entail two contrasting visions of education. Perhaps one of the more profound observations that Lewis makes is that education is inescapably *enculturation*; education is a means by which one is initiated into a culture, into a particular way of being human. For Lewis, the significance of scientific utilitarianism in British education was that it marked the triumphant arrival of the modern age and its assumptions pervading British culture, reconstituting all cultural institutions according to secular rules, understandings, and goals.

But Lewis is not merely a critic of this civilizational shift. He is not a cynical curmudgeon, an "obscurantist" as he himself put it, one who simply laments the death of the old order and the rise of a new one. No, Lewis believes that this propensity, this orientation, toward power and manipulation inherent in the modernist experiment is nothing less than a threat to our humanity as we have known it. If all of reality has been reduced to value-free nature, being understood solely through scientifically defined facts, then even humanity itself will be seen as nothing more than mere nature. And if nature is there to be manipulated to the wants and desires of others, then inevitably the vast majority of humanity will be vulnerable to scientific and technological manipulation according to the needs of a technocratic elite. It is then, when man will have thought he finally conquered nature, that nature will have conquered man, for man as such would cease to exist; a new social order will arise that subsumes the vast majority of humanity under the category of impersonal nature which in effect redefines humanity as inherently meaningless; hence the title of the publication of his lectures, *The Abolition of Man*.

A number of commentators have since echoed Lewis' dire warning. Peter Kreeft observes that *The Abolition of Man* "is a terrifying prophecy of mortality, not just the mortality of modern Western civilization ... but the mortality of human nature itself if we do not recapture belief in [what Lewis calls] the *Tao*, the natural law, the doctrine of objective values."[2] As part of this prophecy of mortality, Lewis identified two fundamental flaws in the modern project that were available for all to see if they would but take a moment to reflect. First, he saw the doubt and skepticism intrinsic to modern epistemology and ethics as inherently self-negating; the secularized standards by which the modern skeptic debunks religious thought and sentiment can just as easily be applied to those very secularized standards. Secondly, he logically traced-out the propensity towards technocratic tyranny inherent in a world governed according to these self-defeating modernist assumptions. Lewis argued that there was only one way to counter and resist these twin futilities: We must turn back to what he calls the *Tao,* the doctrine of objective values, as the only source for what he calls a "regenerate science," and a truly humane vision of life.[3] In Lewis' words: "Only the *Tao* provides a common human law of action which can over-arch rulers and

---

[2] Peter Kreeft, *C.S. Lewis for the Third Millennium: Six Essays on The Abolition of Man* (Ignatius Press: San Francisco, 1994).
[3] Lewis, *Abolition*, 85.

ruled alike. A dogmatic belief in objective value is necessary to the very idea of a rule which is not tyranny or an obedience which is not slavery."[4]

But is this possible? Can we really see a mass *return* in a world so infused with the values of scientific progress and technological advance? Can modern man, who believes he has evolved beyond our infantile past, still heed the summons of Lewis and become as little children, born anew?

I believe the answer to this is an emphatic 'Yes'! I believe we today are in the midst of a mass rebellion against this modernist experiment Lewis so profoundly described; indeed, a recent study on the worldwide resurgence of religion and its challenge to secular modernity was aptly titled *Global Rebellion.* And this rebellion appears to be launching a two-fold front exemplative of Lewis' analysis. On the one hand, postmodernist thought is calling out the self-defeating notion of scientifically-inspired epistemology and ethics, and on the other hand, a renewal of religious nationalism throughout the world is reawakening premodern beliefs and practices as mechanisms of resistance against what are perceived as secularizing, indeed, tyrannizing processes of globalization. And to bring this full circle, in the midst of this global rebellion, we are seeing the renewal of the very classical education that Lewis so ably defended, and with it, the awakening of wisdom and virtue so indispensable to our human flourishing. As such, *The Abolition of Man* does in fact turn out to be a prophecy, not a dire one regarding the mortality of human civilization, but rather the hope of its restoration.

---

[4] Lewis, *Abolition,* 81.

CHAPTER 1

The Postmodern Turn

One of the first indicators that the dominance of scientific rationalism was beginning to wane appeared in 1979, in a book published by the French philosopher and sociologist Jean-François Lyotard entitled *The Postmodern Condition: A Report on Knowledge.* As stated in his opening paragraph, Lyotard argued that since the end of the 1950s and the reconstruction of Europe, the West has been entering into what he calls a *postmodern age.* Lyotard defines 'postmodern' simply as "an incredulity toward metanarratives," a one-size-fits-all vision of knowledge and the world that transcends time and place.[5] Lyotard refers to this condition as *post*modern precisely because he sees a scientific metanarrative at the heart of modernity; moderns consider science and scientific laws as valid for all people, times, and places, such that premodern and religious beliefs and practices have ceded authority to forms of

---

[5] Jean-François Lyotard, *The Postmodern Condition: A Report on Knowledge* (Manchester: Manchester University Press, 1979), xxiv.

truth and reasoning that no longer require religious grounding. The modernization story had hitherto provided the one narrative of progress and competence in relation to which all spheres of Western life had been shaped and defined.

What Lyotard argued was that Western populations had grown increasingly skeptical of this world vision. Instead, he noticed that the modern world was becoming increasingly dominated by a plurality of cultural commitments and lifestyles, with no consensus as to the veracity of any one over the other. As a consequence, the fundamental tenet of modernity, the universality of scientific rationality as the sole objective way of knowing the world, had in effect collapsed in the hearts and minds of most Westerners. Instead, it was increasingly recognized that the scientific metanarrative, the secular claim to absolute and universal truth, was itself nothing more than a mere cultural construct; just one of innumerable life-worlds and cultural commitments. Simply put, the postmodern condition rendered modernity just another culture, nothing more.

The collapse of the modernist metanarrative has grown most evident in the university, particularly in the United States. In his book, *The Decline of the Secular University,* C. John Sommerville argues that the commitment to secularization in the modern research university in effect abandoned the conception of what it means to be human, which of course was C.S. Lewis' chief concern in *The Abolition of Man.* Because the secular entails a materialistic reductionism, questions concerning the nature of what it means to be human have been rendered obsolete. The question itself is simply too religious in nature to be answered by a secularized institution. This loss of human and moral formation in the modern university led to a vacuum, which was filled with the rise of so-called *multiculturalism*, which first made its appearance on American college campuses in the 1960s with the "Third World Movement," a coalition of black, Native American, Asian, and Latino students concerned about the disenfranchisement of racial minorities.[6] As Roger Kimball details in his 1990 study, *Tenured Radicals: How Politics Has Corrupted Our Higher Education,* the traditional literary canon central to the liberal arts vision was increasingly relativized to an expanding literature centered on gender, race, and sexuality. Instead of the masterpieces of Western culture, students at Stanford, for example, could take a class on the Navajos called "Our Bodies, Our Sheep, Our Cosmos, Ourselves."[7]

With the loss of any overarching metanarrative, multicultural theorists began to view personal and institutional relationships through the prism of *power discrepancies.*[8] Take for example the new racial logic that has emerged of late, one that reimagines culture as a binary of antithetical power distributions between a dominant colonialist power (often labeled 'white') that disenfranchises politically and socially minority cultures through sexist, racist, and classist

---

[6] Jenny Sharpe, "Is the United States Postcolonial? Transnationalism, Immigration, and Race," *Diaspora* 4:2 (1995): 181-199, 183.

[7] Roger Kimball, *Tenured Radicals: How Politics Has Corrupted Our Higher Education* (New York: Harper & Row, 1990), 32.

[8] Cf. Jim Leffel, "Postmodernism and 'The Myth of Progress': Two Visions," in Dennis McCallum (ed.), *The Death of Truth: What's Wrong with Multiculturalism, the Rejection of Reason, and the New Postmodern Diversity* (Minneapolis: Bethany House Publishers, 1996), 45.

exclusions. Such a paradigm has forged a new conception of racism specific to systems of power and domination. This 'prejudice plus power' paradigm was well represented by a manual compiled by affirmative action officer Carolyn Pitts in the 1980s, who asserts that in the U.S., "only whites can be racists, since whites dominate and control the institutions that create and enforce American cultural norms and values . . . blacks and other Third World peoples do not have access to the power to enforce any prejudices they may have, so they cannot, by definition, be racists."[9]

Needless to say, the primacy of power in human and institutional relationships leaves little room for the modernist notion of scientific or secularized truth. A recent example of this involved a student response to a letter sent out by the president of Pomona College that reaffirmed their mission as one "founded upon the discovery of truth, the collaborative development of knowledge and the betterment of society." Students subsequently drafted a letter that took issue with the president's commitment to the discovery of truth:

> Historically, white supremacy has venerated the idea of objectivity, and wielded a dichotomy of 'subjectivity vs. objectivity' as a means of silencing oppressed peoples. The idea that there is a single truth– 'the Truth'–is a construct of the Euro-West that is deeply rooted in the Enlightenment, which was a movement that also

---

[9] Cited in Robert Charles Smith, *Racism in the Post-Civil Rights Era: Now You See It, Now You Don't* (Albany, NY: SUNY Press, 1995), 30.

described Black and Brown people as both subhuman and impervious to pain. This construction is a myth ... The idea that the truth is an entity for which we must search, in matters that endanger our abilities to exist in open spaces, is an attempt to silence oppressed peoples.[10]

It is no wonder, then, that in the face of the perceived threat of power discrepancies, multiculturalism is increasingly collapsing into *tribalism,* a danger recognized decades ago by Arthur Schlesinger.[11] As evidenced by the Black Lives Matter movement, La Raza, and what Carol Swaine refers to as the 'new white nationalists,' tribalist sentiments go beyond a mere rejection of the values of modernity, championing a racial and cultural identity that embraces social fission, extreme differentiation, and ethnic-based segmentation.[12]

And yet, in this tribalized rejection of the Enlightenment, postmodernists reveal their own futilities and contradictions. While rejecting the modernist monopoly on truth claims, they ironically accept the modernist redefinition of the world as devoid of any divine meaning and purpose apart from what

---

[10]   http://claremontindependent.com/students-demand-administrators-take-action-against-conservative-journalists/.

[11] In his *The Disuniting of America: Reflections on a Multicultural Society* (New York: Norton, 1991), 58, Schlesinger observed that the acceptance of the tenets of multiculturalism inexorably leads to the "disintegration of the national community, apartheid, Balkanization, [and] tribalization."

[12] Cees Hamelink, "Human Rights: The Next Fifty Years," in Robert Phillipson (ed.), *Rights to Language, Equity, Power and Education* (London: Lawrence Erlbaum Associates, 2000), 63.

cultures chose to impart to it. As such, postmodernists fall prey to the very consequences that Lewis predicted would always occur once the *Tao* is denied. In a world devoid of objective values, all that exists is power and manipulation. Moreover, in rejecting metanarratives in favor of the pursuit of power, postmodernists simply substitute the arbitrariness of the scientific metanarrative with their own. To the extent that current protestors and activists continue to embrace categories and distinctions specific to secularism, they are merely perpetuating the contradictions that toppled their modernist progenitor, thus securing their own eventual overthrow as well.

CHAPTER 2

Globalization and Technocracy

So why do postmodernists reject modernity's truth claims while simultaneously accepting its vision of reality, a world devoid of any divine meaning and purpose? The British sociologist Anthony Giddens sees the postmodern contradiction as the fruit of the phenomenon we call *globalization*. For Giddens, Lyotard's postmodern condition is the result of our collective disillusionment in being caught up within a technological world we don't quite understand, and feel is largely outside of our control.[13] Giddens defines modernity not as a belief system or philosophy, but more as a social order that profoundly influences our vision of the world and our place within it. As a social order, modernity is comprised of the industrialization of material power and machinery, as well as the interaction between a capitalist economy, telecommunications, technology, and mass

---

[13] Anthony Giddens, *The Consequences of Modernity* (Cambridge: Polity Press, 1990), 2-3.

urbanization.[14] In such a complex world, Giddens argues that postmoderns can reject modernity *philosophically* all the while accepting modernity *socially.*

This philosophical/social dichotomy is all the more intensified by globalization, which emerges when this modernist social order extends beyond the West, interweaving transnational and transcontinental levels of human organization into a single political and economic system. At its most basic, globalization involves a pervasive dialectic between the local and the global through a process known as *disembedding.* Disembedding refers to the ways in which our daily routines and practices are no longer defined by their grounding, or embeddedness, in the local context of a restricted *time* and *place.*[15] For example, think about how we tell time today. We all know how time was kept in traditional societies, in accordance with ecology (the perceived position of the sun in the sky) and with rituals that gave such ecological movement its meaning. However, today we keep time with a machine, the mechanical clock; our lives are organized temporally by regulated mechanisms and time zones. This means that the time of, say, noon is the same in Maine as it is in the western most part of Ohio, regardless of the sun's proximity to its meridian for those respective regions. Similarly, the modern age is characterized by disembedded space; whether we are talking about the phone, television, internet, or email, our

---

[14] Anthony Giddens, *Runaway World: How Globalization is Reshaping our Lives* (New York: Routledge, 2000).

[15] Rob Stones, "Disembedding," in George Ritzer (ed.), *The Wiley-Blackwell Encyclopedia of Globalization* (Indianapolis: Wiley, 2012), n.p.

modern society is characterized by processes that transcend localities. Today, we can be closer to someone ten thousand miles away via a cell phone than we are to the person we're sitting next to at Starbucks.

However, disembedding is not limited to time and space; such dislodging also involves localized customs, traditions, languages, and religions, a process known as *detraditionalization.* Modern disembedding involves various secularizing mechanisms by which local customs and traditions are relativized to wider economic, scientific, and technocratic forces.[16] Whereas premodern societies are characterized generally by provincial beliefs and practices considered sacred and absolute, globalized societies offer a range of consumer-based options that call into question the sanctity of local beliefs and practices, relativizing them to a 'global food court' of many other creedal alternatives. As a result, traditional moral codes and customs become increasingly implausible to objectively sustain.

For Giddens, detraditionalizing processes provide moderns with more lifestyle choices than ever, emancipating them from the supposedly arbitrary controls and definitions indicative of traditional societies. As autonomous individuals exercising sovereign control over their own life circumstances, the absolute veracity of a single metanarrative becomes highly improbable. And yet, Giddens' account for the postmodern contradiction itself runs into its own intractable obstacles,

---

[16] Giddens, *Runaway World,* 61-65, 91.

most especially his admission that moderns exercise control over their own lives while simultaneously living in a technocratic world over which they have no control. We may have lots of choices locally, but we're feeling more and more helpless globally.

Indeed, globalization appears to be forging the very two classes of people that Lewis believed inexorably emerge in a world governed by scientific and technological processes, what he called the *conditioners* and the *conditioned*. Globalism is organized around what Giddens calls *expert systems* that operate according to standardized and specialized technical knowledge and protocols.[17] From the building codes embedded in our homes and buildings, to the dependability of our automobiles and the safety of roads and bridges, to air travel, I-phones, etc., we find ourselves increasingly trusting in and indeed dependent upon a class of technological experts for the management of our daily lives. According to Lewis, the danger here is that as more and more people become dependent on technological expertise, technocracies are inevitably ruled by experts and engineers who convince the masses that such competencies are the basis for their freedom and prosperity, a reliance that renders humanity particularly vulnerable to comparable manipulation.

Today, we can see how globalization has reorganized the world around a class of experts who have largely redefined political and economic protocols in the form of a de-facto world

---

[17] Giddens, *Consequences,* 26-28.

government, replete with its own transnational institutions: the European Union, the European Court of Human Rights, the International Monetary Fund (IMF), the World Bank, the G-7, the General Agreement on Tariffs and Trade (GATT), and the like. It is through such world institutions that the modernist West seeks to export the social order distinctive to globalization in the forms of liberal democracy, free markets, and human rights. And with the major alternatives to this global world order – fascism and communism – now dead and buried, scholars such as Francis Fukuyama have postulated that globalism may in fact represent the climatic and inevitable world system of human history.

And yet, the confidence in this brave new world exemplified by the architects and managers of these institutions is not shared by all. As it turns out, this unbridled confidence is beginning to shake. Despite all the globalist rhetoric to the contrary, a very different world is emerging.

CHAPTER 3

The Rise of Nationalist Populism

As sociologist Stjepan Meštrović notes, while Western elites continue to believe that globalism is the unstoppable and inevitable world system of the future, there is in fact nothing short of a global groundswell of resistance against this standardized and mechanist recalibration of the world.[18] What appears to be happening is, through a process known as *segmentary oppositions,* the localized tribalisms forged in the postmodern response to the threat of disproportionate power relations have reconfigured into translocal forms of nationalist and populist sentiments and political organization.[19]

---

[18] Stjepan G. Meštrović, *Anthony Giddens: The Last Modernist* (London/New York: Routledge, 1998).

[19] *Systems of segmentary oppositions* is a term coined by anthropologist E.E. Evans-Pritchard to refer to the ways in which perceived threats form ever expanding coalitions. For example, my brother and I may fight, but then team up to take on the neighbor's kids. But all the kids on the block will team up against kids on another block, and our neighborhood will come together to stand up to another neighborhood, and so on.

In Europe, for example, there has been nothing less than a surge of rightwing and populist parties dedicated to overturning the disembedding effects of globalism and its de-facto one world government. In the past 17 years, the actual number of nationalist and populist parties across the European continent has nearly doubled, growing from 33 to 63.[20] And these parties are seeing extraordinary electoral success. The share of votes won by populist parties in Europe has tripled in the course of such time, from 8.5 percent of the European vote to nearly 25 percent. Since the spring of 2010, there have been over a dozen Parliamentary elections throughout Western Europe, and we can see the electoral surge of nationalist populist parties throughout these elections. In March of 2017, Geert Wilder's Dutch Freedom Party came in second place, a marked difference from 2006 when they came in fifth place. We've seen a comparable surge with the Flemish nationalist and secessionist party in Belgian parliamentary elections, along with the rise of the Swedish Democrats and the anti-European party the True Finns. Marine Le Pen doubled the support of National Front in her recent presidential campaign against the centrist Macron. In Italy, there was a recent mass sweep of center-right candidates winning the vast majority of mayoral elections, with Silvio Berlusconi's Forza Italia party and the anti-immigrant Northern League party trouncing their leftwing rivals by winning over 55 percent of the vote. The so-called Visegrád Four – Hungary, Poland, Slovakia, and the Czech Republic – all have nationalist governments hostile to

---

[20]   https://institute.global/insight/renewing-centre/european-populism-trends-threats-and-future-prospects.

the EU's immigration quotas, a hostility bolstered of late by Austria's electoral turn to the right and the rise of the far-right party Alternative for Germany in their latest rounds of elections.

In the most recent year of elections to date, 2017, the center-left all but collapsed throughout Europe. A total of 946 districts held political elections that year, and the center-left coalitions held their own or improved in a mere 56 districts, or just under six percent of European elections. According to *The Guardian*'s analysis, in almost 94 percent of districts, the center-left lost out to center-right, nationalist or so-called far right parties, as well as populist left parties, which were often as hostile to the Eurozone as the far-right.[21] *The New York Times*' assessment was nothing short of dire: "In most major Western European countries, centre-left parties are in retreat, and in some cases they have practically ceased to exist."[22]

What accounts for this mass global rebellion against the technocratic promises of globalization? There appear to be at least two interconnected dynamics propelling this blowback. On the one hand, there is an increasing consensus among non-Western nations that globalism represents nothing less than a foreign invasion, a kind of invasive cultural imperialism.[23] And as phrases such as "the bullies in Brussels" in European

---

[21] https://www.theguardian.com/politics/ng-interactive/2017/dec/29/2017-and-the-curious-demise-of-europes-centre-left.

[22] https://www.nytimes.com/2017/12/28/opinion/germany-social-democrats-coalition.html.

[23] See the discussion in John Anderson, *Conservative Christian Politics in Russia and the United States: Dreaming of Christian Nations* (London: Routledge, 2015).

populist rhetoric evidences, even Western nations are accusing institutions such as the European Union of totalitarian tendencies.[24] And, on the other hand, these power discrepancies are exasperated by what Cornell sociologist Mabel Berezin has identified as three *insecurities* inherent in globalized dynamics.[25] Berezin notes that the nation-state historically promised to provide secure borders, a stable economy, and the space for the celebration and perpetuation of a population's customs, traditions, and religion. But as Berezin observes, these three securities have eroded as the result of dynamics inherent in globalization.[26]

First, because the constituents of globalization, such as transnational corporations and electronic money, transcend national borders, many scholars believe that globalization is bringing an end to the whole concept of distinct nations. And as Paul Harris has observed, these porous borders which serve to expedite flows of goods within a globalized economy entail a significant increase in levels of immigration, both legal and

---

[24] Cf. Janet Daley, "The EU still hasn't understood that it is a totalitarian institution," http://www.telegraph.co.uk/news/2016/09/17/the-eu-still-hasnt-understood-that-it-is-a-totalitarian-institut/.

[25] Mabel Berezin, "The Normalization of the Right in Post-Security Europe," in Armin Schäfer and Wolfgang Streeck (eds.), *Politics in the Age of Austerity* (Cambridge: Polity Press, 2013), 239-61.

[26] Mabel Berezin, "Globalization Backlash," http://people.soc.cornell.edu/mmb39/Forthcoming%20Globalization%20B acklash.pdf.

illegal.[27] Moreover, the threat of terrorism only exaggerates the anxieties over the porous borders, rendering border insecurities a seemingly permanent part of our political and national landscapes.

Secondly, globalization tends to negate local industry with a global division of labor that relocates manufacturing to the global South, while finance and ownership of capital has coalesced around the West. As a result, the last few decades have been characterized by a mass exodus of industrial and manufacturing jobs from the U.S. and Western Europe into so-called third world or global South nations such as Mexico and China. The economic collapse of 2008 hit Europe hard, but particularly the young. Net employment in the eurozone fell by about 6 million between 2008 and 2013, and half of those affected were under the age of 25. It's hardly surprising that millennials' confidence in the European Union and for economic integration has imploded; for example, in Spain, only about 30 percent of youth support the EU, while in Italy it's down to just 12 percent.

Thirdly, border and economic insecurities are rivaled by ontological or cultural insecurity. We noted above that one of the consequences of the disembedding dynamics in globalization is what scholars call detraditionalization. Once social life is caught up in a global industrialized economic system, it is propelled away from traditional, national, and

---

[27] Paul A. Harris, "Immigration, Globalization and National Security: An Emerging Challenge to the Modern Administrative State," http://unpan1.un.org/intradoc/groups/public/documents/aspa/unpan0063 51.pdf.

local practices and beliefs. As a result, traditional moral codes and cultural customs become increasingly implausible to objectively sustain, and populations increasingly sense that the beliefs and practices so central to their historic cultural identity are withering away.

And so, as Berezin concludes, the globalized emergence of these insecurities has provided the political context and climate in which nationalist populist solutions to political issues appear plausible and normal. And this rightward turn is hardly limited to Europe. Studies of the Israeli electorate found that elections held within a few months of a terrorist attack caused an increase in support of the political right, even within left-leaning localities.[28] Another study detailed how repeated exposure to rocket threats shifted Israeli voter support to rightwing nationalists during the 2003-9 elections.[29] A comparable turn towards nationalist parties has been observed in Turkey in response to attacks by Kurdish PKK militants.[30]

Similarly, a recent article entitled "2016 was the Year of the Wall" reluctantly admits that the global right is successfully tightening borders throughout the world.[31] They cite India's border with Pakistan and Bangladesh, Israel/Palestine, and

---

[28] "Are Voters Sensitive to Terrorism? Direct Evidence from the Israeli Electorate," *American Political Science Review* Vol. 102, No. 3 (August 2008): 279-301.
[29] "Terrorism and Voting: The Effect of Rocket Threat on Voting in Israeli Elections," Vol. 108, No. 3 (August 2014): 588-604.
[30] https://politicalviolenceataglance.org/2015/11/23/divide-and-conquer-the-long-term-political-effects-of-terrorism/.
[31] https://thinkprogress.org/2016-was-the-year-of-the-wall-bb063fa19061/.

Saudi Arabia/Yemen, along with the border walls in France, Hungary, Austria, Italy, and Greece. It appears as if everywhere we look, border walls are going up, they're not coming down. And far from being 'Berlin walls,' they tend to be built around sentiments that seek to protect culture, religion, tradition, language, land, and custom.

Thus, for a number of scholars, globalism is not inevitable; quite the contrary: everywhere we look, more and more, the world is turning to the nationalist populist right.

CHAPTER 4

Retraditionalization and the Resurgence of Religion

The three insecurities identified by Berezin leads us to perhaps the most significant development in this mass turn to the right: In the face of threats to a sense of place, identity, and security, populations tend to reassert historic identity and security markers, such as religion, custom, and tradition as mechanisms of resistance against secular globalization's anti-cultural anti-traditional dynamics. Or in Kinnvall's words: "As individuals feel vulnerable and experience existential anxiety, it is not uncommon for them to wish to reaffirm a threatened self-identity. Any collective identity that can provide such security is a potential pole of attraction."[32]

---

[32] Catarina Kinnvall, "Globalization and Religious Nationalism: Self, Identity, and the Search for Ontological Security," *Political Psychology* Vol. 25, No. 5 (Oct., 2004): 741-767, 742.

As a result, the anti-traditionalist dynamics inherent in globalization have elicited what scholars are calling *retraditionalization*, a renewed interest in "traditions of wisdom that have proved their validity through the test of history," or "a longing for spiritual traditions and practices that have stood the test of time, and therefore can be valued as authentic resources for spiritual renewal."[33] With post-security polity as our backdrop, the important point here is that retraditionalization is not limited simply to spiritual renewal or religious revival; it often involves a reconfiguration of political, cultural, and educational norms around pre-modern religious beliefs and practices as a response to the secularizing processes of globalization.[34]

Examples of retraditionalization abound:

In Russia, reference has been made to the notion of *spiritual security* as a subset of national security in a number of policy documents issued by the Putin government.[35] In 2000, the National Security Concept of Russia stated that the assurance of the Russian Federation's national security included protecting the nation's cultural, spiritual, and moral legacy and the historical traditions and standards of public life. Spiritual security accounts for the astonishing rise to prominence

---

[33] Leif Gunnar Engedal, "*Homo Viator.* The Search for Identity and Authentic Spirituality in a Post-modern Context," in Kirsi Tirri (ed.) *Religion, Spirituality and Identity* (Bern: Peter Lang, 2006), 45-64, 58.

[34] Ivan Varga, "Detraditionalization and Retraditionalization," in Mark Juergensmeyer and Wade Clark Roof (eds.), *Encyclopedia of Global Religion* (Los Angeles: Sage Publications, 2012), 295-98, 297.

[35] Julie Elkner, "Spiritual Security in Putin's Russia," available at http://historyandpolicy.org/papers/ policy-paper-26.html.

experienced by the Russian Orthodox Church. John Burgess' recent study documents how, after its near complete decimation under the communist regime, the Church has grown to more than thirty-five thousand parishes, eight hundred monasteries, and innumerable welfare and educational ministries spread throughout the nation.[36] The most recent surveys corroborate that nearly 70 percent of the Russian population see themselves as either religious or very religious, and an astonishing 93 percent affirm their support and respect for the Russian Orthodox Church and Orthodox Christians. A recent survey even found that 30 percent of Russians would like to see a return to some kind of monarchical rule comparable to the Tsars.

We're seeing the rise of religious nationalism particularly in India with the mass electoral success of the BJP or the Bharatiya Janata Party, which is the right-wing party of India, and the largest democratic political party in the world. The party's leader and the current prime-minister, Narendra Modi, comes from a Hindu nationalist group that explicitly seeks to reorganize the Indian nation, society, and culture around conservative Hindu beliefs and practices.

In Central Europe, Poland held a Catholic mass aired on national television in November of 2016 declaring Jesus Christ as King and Lord over their nation in the presence of Prime Minister Andrzej Duda. Prime Minister Viktor Orban in

---

[36] John P. Burgess, *Holy Rus': The Rebirth of Orthodoxy in the New Russia* (New Haven: Yale University Press, 2017).

Hungary is championing the defense of Christian civilization over against the secular globalization represented by the European Union; Eastern European nations such as Georgia have reintroduced Orthodox Christianity back into their public-school curriculum. In Turkey, a number of scholars have noted that both President Erdoğan and his party, the AKP or Justice and Development Party, are interested in transforming the once secular democratic republic into a neo-Anatolian federation of Muslim ethnicities, a transformation that may even involve a revived caliphate.

In the Pacific, the parliament of Samoa recently declared the island a Christian nation with a constitution dedicated to the Holy Trinity; there's a revival of imperial Shintoism at the highest levels of the Japanese government, a revitalization of Confucian philosophy among Chinese officials, we could go on and on and on. Indeed, sociologist Rodney Stark argues that we are currently in the midst of the single greatest religious surge the world has ever seen.[37] According to the authors of *God's Century,* traditional religions throughout the world "enjoy *greater capacity for political influence* today than at any time in modern history – and perhaps ever."[38]

As it turns out, postmodern sensibilities appear particularly prone towards resolving their innate paradoxes in retraditionalization. Because the postmodern notion of truth is

---

[37] Rodney Stark, *The Triumph of Faith: Why the World is More Religious than Ever* (Wilmington, DE: ISI Books, 2015).
[38] Monica Duffy Toft, Daniel Philpott, Timothy Samuel Shah, *God's Century: Resurgent Religion and Global Politics* (New York: Norton and Company, 2011), 49, emphasis original.

open and unfixed, the experience of sacred and divine reality is fully within the realm of possibility; and because identity is fluid, a postmodern world finds such an experience in its traditional forms highly desirable, especially in terms of how it might overcome the extreme fragmentation of postmodern life with meaningful commitments and integration.[39] Indeed, it thus appears that the twin-futilities of the modern experiment identified by Lewis – its epistemological/ethical incoherence and its propensity towards technocratic tyranny – are both ultimately resisted in a convergence around retraditionalization.

---

[39] Engedal, "*Homo Viator,*" 58.

CHAPTER 5

A Demographic Revolution

The implications of this retraditionalization for the 21st century are frankly incalculable. Take, for example, the latest findings in demography. According to University of London scholar Eric Kaufmann's detailed study on global demographic trends, we are in the early stages of nothing less than a demographic revolution. In Kaufmann's words, "religious fundamentalists are on course to take over the world."[40] This is because there is a significant demographic deficit between secularists and conservative religionists. For example, in the U.S., while self-identified non-religionist women averaged only 1.5 children per couple, conservative evangelical women averaged 2.5 children, representing a 28 percent fertility edge. Kaufmann notes that this demographic deficit has dramatic effects over time. In a population evenly divided, these numbers indicate that conservative evangelicals would

---

[40] Eric Kaufmann, *Shall the Religious Inherit the Earth? Demography and Politics in the Twenty-First Century* (London: Profile Books, 2010), ix.

increase from 50 to 62.5 percent of the population in a single generation. In two generations, their number would increase to 73.5 percent, and over the course of 200 years, they would represent 99.4 percent. The Amish and Mormons provide contemporary illustrations of the compound effect of endogamous growth. The Amish double in population every twenty years, and projections have the Amish numbering over a million in the U.S. and Canada in just a few decades. Since 1830, Mormon growth has averaged 40 percent per decade, which means that by 2080, there may be as many as 267 million Mormons in the world, making them by 2100 anywhere from one to six percent of the world's population.

In Europe, immigration has ironically made the continent *more* religiously conservative, not less; in fact, London and Paris are some of the most religiously dense areas within their respective populations. In Britain, for example, Ultra-Orthodox or Haredi Jews constitute only 17 percent of the Jewish population but account for 75 percent of Jewish births. And in Israel, Haredi schoolchildren have gone from comprising a few percent to nearly a third of all Jewish pupils in a matter of five decades, and are poised to represent the majority of the Jewish population by 2050. Since 1970, charismatic Christians in Europe have expanded steadily at a rate of 4 percent per year, in step with Muslim growth. Currently, Laestadian Lutherans in Finland and Holland's Orthodox Calvinists have a fertility advantage over their wider secular populations of 4:1 and 2:1 respectively.

In contrast, Kaufmann's data projects that secularists, who consistently exemplify a low fertility rate of around 1.5 (significantly below the replacement level of 2.1), will begin a steady decline after 2030 to a mere 14 to 15 percent of the American population. Similar projections apply to Europe as well. Kaufmann thus appears to have identified what he calls "the soft underbelly of secularism," namely, demography.[41] This is because secular liberalism entails its own "demographic contradiction," the affirmation of the sovereign individual devoid of the restraints of classical moral structures *necessitates* the freedom not to reproduce. The link between sex and procreation having been broken, modernist reproduction translates into mere personal preference. It thus turns out that the radical individualism so celebrated and revered by contemporary secular propagandists is in fact the agent by which their ideology implodes.

Lewis certainly had a sense of this, particularly as it pertained to the modern use of and attitudes toward contraception. Absent the doctrine of objective values, the conquest over nature entails the conquest over *human* nature; as scientific manipulation has reduced reality to nature, man himself becomes merely a byproduct of nature *and therefore a legitimate object of control*. This is how Lewis understood modern contraception, where earlier generations in effect exercise control over later ones.[42] However, as Kaufmann has demonstrated, this calculus is turning out to be just another factor in secular modernity's demise.

---

[41] Kaufmann, *Shall the Religious*, xv.
[42] Lewis, *Abolition*, 67.

CHAPTER 6

The Return of Classical Education

Indeed, with the revitalization of pro-natal sentiments among conservative Christians throughout the globe, we come full circle with Lewis' concerns in *The Abolition of Man,* which centered on the nature of education and its role in initiating students into a particular cultural vision of what it means to be human. For at the heart of retraditionalization particularly here in the States, we are seeing nothing less than a renaissance of the very education to which Lewis summoned our return.

According to the Association of Classical Christian Schools' membership statistics, there were 10 classical schools in the nation in 1994, today there are over 230. Since 2002, student enrollment in classical schools has more than doubled from 17,000 nationwide to over 41,000. And these are just ACCS affiliated schools. There are estimates that classical Christian schools now number upwards of over 500 in the nation.

Classical homeschool organizations such as Classical Conversations have also thrived, with a current student enrollment of over 60,000. And again, there are estimates that the number of home-school children who receive a classical education may be ten times larger than their conventional peers.

We're also seeing among Catholic schools a mass shift towards rediscovering anew the ancient or traditional way of approaching education. A recent example involves an entire diocese of schools in Michigan who have rejected Common Core by returning to a distinctively Catholic liberal arts education. Moreover, we're seeing the development of networks and organizations such as the Institute for Catholic Liberal Education and annual conferences that are providing the professional development necessary for a vibrant faculty and administration.

The charter school movement as well, now representing 10 percent of publicly funded schools, is becoming fertile ground for classical education. The Great Hearts Academies operates currently 25 public charter schools in Arizona and Texas, which together enroll 13,000 students with another 13,000 on waiting lists.[43] The Barney Initiative of Hillsdale College has the second-largest network of public classical schools, serving over six thousand students spanning seven states. Altogether, the total number of classical charter schools may be upwards of 150 in the nation.

And we are already seeing the effects of this kind of education. As of 2015, classically educated students had the highest SAT

---

[43] John J. Miller, "Back to Basics," *National Review* Vol. 67 Issue 19 (October 2015): 42-44.

scores in each of the three categories of Reading, Math, and Writing among all independent, religious, and public schools. In fact, even the SAT and ACT are being rivaled by the advent of the CLT or the Classical Learning Test, an evaluation far more reflective of a classical and Christian education than what is represented by contemporary standardized testing. This represents I think the beginning of a real transformation in education assessment that has profound implications for what we consider to be an educated person in an increasingly post-secular world. The CLT resembles other standardized tests, but it breaks the area of verbal reasoning down into four sub areas: philosophy/religion, natural science, literature, and historical/founding documents. Though only a couple of years old, over 90 colleges have agreed to accept the scores for the CLT instead of the SAT and the ACT, and more than 300 high schools across the country are serving as centers for CLT testing.

But more than all of this, the renaissance of classical education is once again placing wisdom and virtue at the center of educational renewal. As Lewis noted, "Until quite modern times, all teachers and even all men believed the universe to be such that certain emotional reactions on our part could be either congruous or incongruous to it—believed, in fact, that objects did not merely receive, but could *merit*, our approval or disapproval, our reverence, or our contempt."[44] He then summons some of history's greatest minds as witnesses to such a view of the world. In particular, he cites Augustine's

---

[44] Lewis, *Abolition,* 27-8.

conception of virtue as *ordo amoris,* the right ordering of our loves. Augustine is drawing from a similar tradition as Aristotle, who defines education as teaching the student to like and dislike what he ought. And such well-trained dispositions lead to a virtuous life. So, too, Plato in his *Republic,* who writes that the well-nurtured youth is one who loves what is truly lovely and desires what is truly desirable.

In light of this larger retraditionalization dynamic, it is no coincidence that we are seeing a return to precisely this vision of education. We are once again cultivating wisdom in teaching students to discern the divine economy of goods, seeing the world analogous to how God sees it; and in turn, we are cultivating virtue by learning to conform our loves and desires with just such a divine economy. As such, the current classical renewal represents a move beyond mere tribalist and nationalist blowbacks; we are seeing nothing less than a return of the education for a flourishing humanity and the realization of Lewis' hope: the restoration of man.

CONCLUSION

The Triumph of Tradition

I do not pretend to know C.S. Lewis' mind on these matters, whether he specifically portended the demise of the secular age. But he did identify two fundamental futilities in modernity that have since turned out to be fatal to its vision of knowledge and ethics along with its technocratically-inspired world order. And I can't help but think he had a sense of how things would in fact transpire in the future.

I've recently developed a renewed appreciation of the final volume of Lewis' Space Trilogy entitled *That Hideous Strength.* In the Preface, Lewis described the story as a fictional depiction of the ideas he developed in *The Abolition of Man*. Subtitled *A Modern Fairy-Tale for Grown Ups, That Hideous Strength* was published in 1945 but finished just a few months after he delivered the threefold lectures in Durham; so, we know that Lewis was writing this story when he delivered these lectures. As anticipated by the third and last chapter of *Abolition, That Hideous Strength* is a novel that explores what the world would be like if it was ruled by a technocratic elite no longer restrained by traditional values and morality.

The title borrows a line from the sixteenth-century poem by Sir David Lyndsay that describes the original Tower of Babel; as such, Lewis reveals his interpretation of the secularizing dynamics in the modern age. For Lewis, this eclipse of religion and virtue by the rise of a Babel-like scientific technocracy is ultimately a spiritual battle between angels and demons, the forces of light and truth against those of darkness and deception. Lewis did not view our modern scientific age as merely the latest chapter of inevitable progress and societal evolution; this was and remains a deeply spiritual battle, where the powers and principalities of the world become incarnate through a scientific priesthood that seek to conform the totality of physical and psychological life around themselves.

But this technocratic tyranny is ultimately defeated, and it's no coincidence how it is vanquished: It is through the intervention of King Arthur's heir, Ransom, and the resuscitation of Merlin's body that had been lying buried in a timeless state, and his cursing of the leaders of the technocracy; thus, the modern age is ultimately defeated by a *return,* the reawakening of a pre-modern world, a classical medieval world that is not dead but lying in a timeless state, waiting to rise again.

Similarly, retraditionalization is awakening all over the world, bringing to the fore pre-modern beliefs and practices that are challenging the dominance of modernity. As it turns out, we *can* return; we *can* go back. On the one hand, postmodernist thought is calling out the self-defeating notion of scientifically-inspired epistemology and ethics, and on the other hand, a renewal of religious nationalism is arousing premodern beliefs and practices as mechanisms of resistance against the anti-cultural processes of globalization and its secular aristocracy, all the while affording the opportunity for an educational renaissance, precisely the kind championed by Lewis as necessary for a flourishing humanity. Standing at the dawn of the 21st century, we can see that Lewis' warning and wish have come together; *The Abolition of Man* does in fact turn out to be a prophecy, not one regarding the mortality of a truly human civilization, but rather its recovery, its renewal, indeed its reawakening.

Thank you again for purchasing this book!

I hope this book encouraged you by showing you all the ways the world is becoming more and more conservative.

If you enjoyed this book, then I'd like to ask you for a favor: Would you be kind enough to leave a review for this book on Amazon? I would so greatly appreciate it!

Thank you so much, and may God richly bless you!

Steve Turley

www.turleytalks.com

Check Out My Other Books

Below you'll find some of my other popular books that are popular on Amazon. Simply go to the links below to check them out. Alternatively, you can visit my author page on Amazon to see my other works.

- *Classical vs. Modern Education: A Vision from C.S. Lewis* http://amzn.to/2opDZju

- *Gazing: Encountering the Mystery of Art* https://amzn.to/2yKi6k9

- *Beauty Matters: Creating a High Aesthetic in School Culture* https://amzn.to/2L8Ejd7

- *Ever After: How to Overcome Cynical Students with the Role of Wonder in Education* http://amzn.to/2jbJI78

- *Movies and the Moral Imagination: Finding Paradise in Films* http://amzn.to/2zjghJj

- *Health Care Sharing Ministries: How Christians are Revolutionizing Medical Cost and Care* http://amzn.to/2B2Q8B2

- *The Face of Infinite of Love: Athanasius on the Incarnation* http://amzn.to/2oxULNM

- *President Trump and Our Post-Secular Future: How the 2016 Election Signals the Dawning of a Conservative Nationalist Age* http://amzn.to/2B87Q22

- *Stressed Out: Learn How an Ancient Christian Practice Can Relieve Stress and Overcome Anxiety* http://amzn.to/2kFzcpc

- *Wise Choice: Six Steps to Godly Decision Making* http://amzn.to/2qy3C2Z

- *Awakening Wonder: A Classical Guide to Truth, Goodness, and Beauty* http://amzn.to/2ziKR5H

- *Worldview Guide for* A Christmas Carol http://amzn.to/2BCcKHO

- *The Ritualized Revelation of the Messianic Age: Washings and Meals in Galatians and 1 Corinthians* http://amzn.to/2B0mGvf

If the links do not work, for whatever reason, you can simply search for these titles on the Amazon website to find them.

About www.TurleyTalks.com

Are we seeing the revitalization of Christian civilization?

For decades, the world has been dominated by a process known as globalization, an economic and political system that hollows out and erodes a culture's traditions, customs, and religions, all the while conditioning populations to rely on the expertise of a tiny class of technocrats for every aspect of their social and economic lives.

Until now.

All over the world, there's been a massive blowback against the anti-cultural processes of globalization and its secular aristocracy. From Russia to Europe and now in the U.S., citizens are rising up and reasserting their religion, culture, and nation as mechanisms of resistance against the dehumanizing tendencies of secularism and globalism.

And it's just the beginning.

The secular world is at its brink, and a new traditionalist age is rising.

Join me each week as we examine these worldwide trends, discover answers to today's toughest challenges, and together learn to live in the present in light of even better things to come.

So hop on over to www.TurleyTalks.com and have a look around. Make sure to sign-up for our weekly Email Newsletter where you'll get lots of free giveaways, private Q&As, and tons of great content. Check out our YouTube channel (www.youtube.com/c/DrSteveTurley) where you'll understand current events in light of conservative trends to help you flourish in your personal and professional life. And of course, 'Like' us on Facebook and follow us on Twitter.

Thank you so much for your support and for your part in this cultural renewal.

About the Author

Steve Turley (PhD, Durham University) is an internationally recognized scholar, speaker, and classical guitarist. He is the author of over a dozen books, including *Classical vs. Modern Education: A Vision from C.S. Lewis, Awakening Wonder: A Classical Guide to Truth, Goodness, and Beauty*, and *The Ritualized Revelation of the Messianic Age: Washings and Meals in Galatians and 1 Corinthians*. Steve broadcasts on current events and cultural trends at TurleyTalks.com. He is a faculty member at Tall Oaks Classical School in Bear, DE, where he teaches Theology and Rhetoric, and Professor of Fine Arts at Eastern University. Steve lectures at universities, conferences, and churches throughout the U.S. and abroad. His research and writings have appeared in such journals as *Christianity and Literature, Calvin Theological Journal, First Things, Touchstone*, and *The Chesterton Review*. He and his wife, Akiko, have four children and live in Newark, DE, where they together enjoy fishing, gardening, and watching *Duck Dynasty* marathons.

Made in the USA
Monee, IL
24 October 2021

80001557R00033